OVERWHELMED

JANE SCHROEDER

"OVERWHELMED"
Copyright © 2022

This edition published in 2022 by Seraph Creative
ISBN 978-1-922428-92-9

Written by Jane Schroeder
www.janeschroeder.com

Illustrations and edited by Melanie van der Linde

Cover Illustration by Rebecca Morris
RebeccaMorris Art

Layout Design by Lizzie Masters, Studio Nebula
lizzie.studionebula@gmail.com

All rights reserved. No part of this publication may be reproduced, stored in a retrieval system or transmitted, in any form or by any means, electronic, mechanical, photocopying, recording or otherwise, without the prior permission of the copyright holder. Scripture quotations are from the New King James Verison unless otherwise marked.

All rights reserved. No part of this book, artwork included may be used or reproduced in any manner without the written permission of the publisher.

Copyright © 2022 Jane Schroeder
jjane.schroeder@gmail.com

OVERWHELMED

JANE SCHROEDER

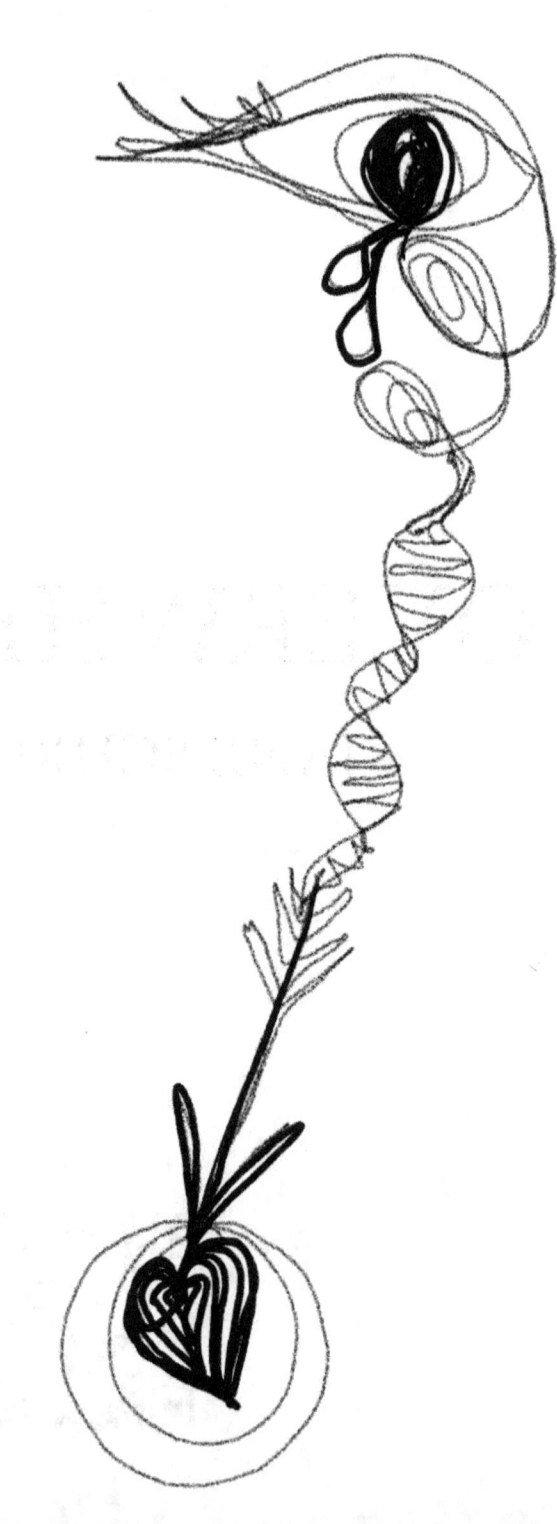

HAND PICKED

In childlike innocence,
Before the dawn of time
I was handpicked by God himself, the creator,
A target of His Love,

Bulls eye!

Grafted into the tapestry of Love.

Divine umbilical cord,
Conductor between heaven and earth.
Pipe song of embryo fullness,

Respiratory joy!

Dipping,
      Diving,
           Swimming,
                Swirling,

Water flumes of life source.
Gateway of formation imagination,
Mainlined in His strength,
Nourishment of sound.

Life Sustenance!
Life existence, sustained, our daily bread.
Jesus Christ!
Bull's eye,

Respiratory Joy!

Life,
    Sustenance,
        Existence,
           Nourished,

Quenches my thirst,
In the dry parched land.

CRYSTAL SEA

Walk hand in hand along the crystal sea,
Terrorforming creation's glow of groaning sounds
whispering free,

A summer breeze on the tinkering turquoise bluish green.
Lapping sounds though clear crystal hue,

Paddling toes in salty sea's,
Tiddler fish great and small enjoy the gaiety.

Delighting in the Creator of light,
A sunbathing sideways crab bathing, pinchers ready to
devour.

LAZY DAISY

White daisy heads, honey bees, rustic orange-red admirals fluttering wings.

Windy walks on doggie trails, Hawthorne bushes bursting bountiful blackberry fruit, all juicy stained fingerprints.

Wild raspberries doted here and there through prickly stems, tiny red droplets hang waiting to be plucked.

Copper skillet boiled, hot syrupy sugary aromas of apple berry jam drift.

UNDONE

I am in love with Him… with God.
He is always on my mind.
From the depths of my soul, I dream about Him.
Hope for mankind.

I think about Him, dream about Him.
He's always on my mind.
My Lord thinks about me, dreams about me.
Because I am always on His mind.

God is in love with me.
He reveals to me His heart.
Whispering to me His mysteries of Love,
I say yes, I know Your Love will never depart.

You move my heart with sweet Bliss.
Piercing my very will,
My reason to live and love again.
I look up, and You are there, still.

Walking in the Spirit, day by day,
Wrapped in Your loving cloud
Undone in Your sweet embrace
There's no greater comfort to be found.

You unravel my heart in Love.
As You desire to be with me.
Longing for the day to make all things new.
I say yes, I surrender to Your sovereignty.

I was born to be with You.
You transform me with Your blood transfusion
Into reflections of Your light being,
A mystical union.

Luminous, radiating diamond skin.
Light being of Your Love.
Breath of God dripping from honeydew lips.
In common union, born from above.

Every cell absorbing transforming Love.
Pulsating, though my veins,
I am undone, raptured, ravished.
Beyond comprehension, in me, Your Love reigns.

I am caught up into paradise,
As you play the strings of my heart.
On the Earth or in the spirit? I do not know.
In my body, or out?

All I desire is to behold Your beauty.
As you call me to Your grave.
The mysterious depths of Your irresistible love.
Your iridescent radiating face.

A warm, liquid tear escapes my eye,
As sorrow begins to flow
With the sweet gushing from your side,
My blood, or Yours? I do not know.

Swallowed in a golden liquid stream.
From the depths of abiding
Here, in the epicenter of your heart,
Joy has come! It's a beautiful morning.

No more wearied enveloping weakness.
Look! Fresh bread, manna.
Once more, the desire overwhelms me,
I surrender.

I am in Love with Him, with God
He is always on my mind.
My Lord thinks about me, dreams about me.
Because I am always on His mind.

BEACH HEAD WALKS WITH MY FATHER

Amidst folk law tales of dragon's lair.
Small bunny rabbits roam
Wild and free
On grassland beauty deity.

Creation says:
"Come play with me,
Let's slide,
Down the fiery tails of Seraphim."

Who's darts pierce to my very soul,
Heart to kill,
Burning passion
Prevents the drill.

I look up, there on its Beach Head throne,
Sits the Seraphim
With blazing rule,
Mountains melt like wax before it's flame

Lightening flashing all about its deity
Perched on Irvine hill,
Staring out to sea
With its burning will.

The hummingbirds fly high above,
The eagles soar,
A red kite swoops from hatched babies' nest
All fluffy feathered from mummy's breast.

Under the shield of him who knows best, Abba Father.
I hear the sound of distant lands roaring
Deep cries out to deep,
Celestial sounds boom far and wide.

Blue cloudy inky skies,
Faces shine forth on crystal seas of glass.
Irvine green fresh river upon the estuary of sound.
A frequency of ecstasy,

Green and pleasant land,
Oh, bonny Scotland
Oh, brave you are
Thy beauty shines for all to see

In your ruggedness, you rally forth your troops,
Where stains of Love have strewn the land
It cries for vengeance
Urgency.

Oh, fiery breath!
The piercing heart of rainbow colours
Rainbow seas.
We smell your burning heather roots

The gorse all prickly
Crown of thorns,
Did such Love and sorrow ever meet?
Demands my life my soul my all.

In silence, stillness underground.
Moles burrow, interconnecting, feasting
On their wormy captives
Eaten alive.

Freedom is our daily bread.
We are not dead.
In Yahweh we live
Our life source complete,

Frequency of sound
We breathe again,
Alive in His immense, entwining benevolence,
Awakened.

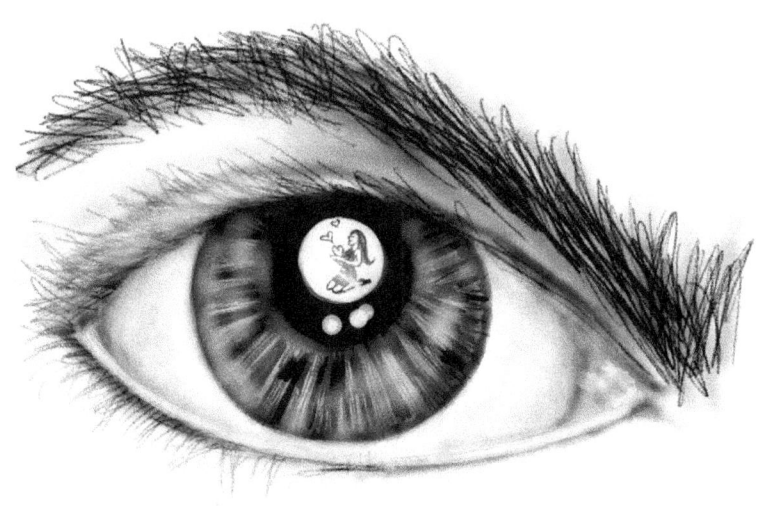

GAZE

Your eyes are on me always
You never break your gaze
Above the mighty waters
I gaze upon your face

Oh, how I love you
You never break your gaze
Your Love is irresistible
You over-shadow me, always

I will gaze upon Your beauty
As I behold Your face
Radiant rainbow kaleidoscope
I will never break my gaze

I will never look away
My heart swells in my chest
Bursting with passionate Love
A bond-servant of Jesus

A CUP OF JOY
A CUP OF SUFFERING

Twisted body, blood saturated matted hair.
Love and valour flow mingled down.
Agonising ripped jagged wounded palms.
His furrowed brow pieced with a thorny crown.

Crimson tide of sticky liquid Love.
Nailed feet of burnished bronze, gouged,
Dripping flesh wounds from saturated white hem
Father saw Him scourged.

Swooning in Messiah's presence
I faint as the sight of such glory,
Clothed in His death and resurrection,
Baptised into Sweet Union, so Holy

Oh, what a glorious transfiguration,
A brand-new world, a brand-new nation!

NEWBIES

Ireland's beauty stands tall and free.
Long term friendship, family.
Newborn babies, future kings,
David, Arthur, Judah, Atlas, treasury.

Raise the Nations to former glory
Kingdoms become our legacy.
Oh, fair lands of Bards and Picts,
Decree sapphire pavements destiny.

Embedded clover spread afar,
Green pastures, Celtic knots.
A white striped dream arises.
The sound of golden harps.

Come let's dance…
as if no one were watching,
Together let's sing…
as if no one were listening.

BLUE BLUE

Arthur blue eyed baby boy.
Crown of England brave and true,
Honour is the name of your game.
Blue, Blue we love you.

Sovereign prince fairest in the land.
Sun-kissed shores of grace
Sunflower blooming, salty seas,
Pearl drop stream reflecting your face.

Blue-green cascading waterfalls
Destiny dreams of future trees
Born to be king, born to sing.
Declarations over land and sea.

Blue, Blue we love you,
A true blue-eyed baby boy.
Christ formation, transformation
Burning Blue for all to enjoy.

True blue we love you Blue eyed-baby boy.

SILENCE

In this place of groaning from
the deep darkness within,
Words become futile

My heart misses a beat
As it pounds in union with His
Sweet enjoyment of Oneness bliss.

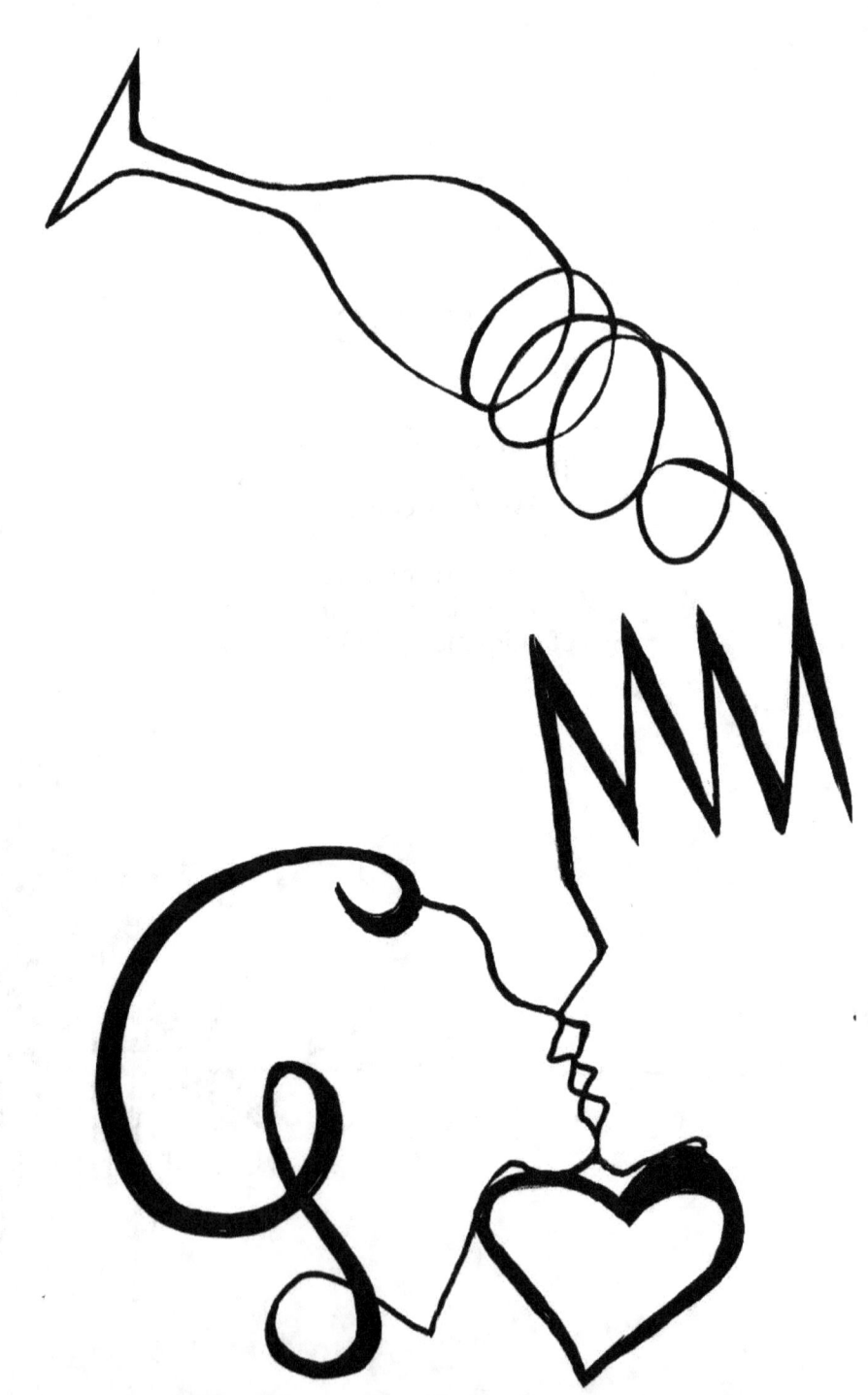

WHERE JUSTICE LIVES

Rumbling In the thunder, the frequency of laughter
From the Courts of Grace
Swirling in the wine in the rhythm of time
Chariots of Joy take their place.

Crashing in the breakers, in the waves of light
Lady Justice Takes her seat.
In the Treasure Rooms of Destiny's Delight
Ancient Wisdom and sacred blood meet

Trumpet sounds of Mercy and Grace.
Life prevails as we meet him face to face.

REALMS

I came up
through a flaming sword
swirling in letters of light.

I came up
through a singing river
breathing air of water

I came up
through a golden garden
a fortress of a name.

I came up
though arms of fiery spirals
of unbreakable might

I came up
through a living fountain
of unceasing Love

KALEIDOSCOPE

Seven flames combined
As I look into bright mantles,
Of Holy

Mingled fire dancing
As I stand upon a lucid sea,
Of Reality

Now I understand
As it gushes from fiery hues
Of Spirit burning

Jane Schroeder is a passionate lover of Yeshua who continues to dive deeper and deeper into the mystery and riches of the Blood of Christ and the glory of His suffering. It overflows and influences every verse penned within these pages.

www.ingramcontent.com/pod-product-compliance
Lightning Source LLC
Chambersburg PA
CBHW070341120526
44590CB00017B/2972